3-6-9, 12 Manifestation Journal

3-6-9, 12 Manifestation Journal

Matthew Petchinsky

3 69, 12 Manifestation Journal
By: Matthew Petchinsky

Introduction to the 369 Manifestation Method

The 369 Manifestation Method is a powerful and transformative practice that utilizes the energy of repetition, focus, and intention to help individuals attract their deepest desires into their reality. Rooted in numerology and popularized by the teachings of Nikola Tesla, this method has gained widespread attention for its simplicity and effectiveness in the world of manifestation. Tesla himself famously stated, "If you only knew the magnificence of the numbers 3, 6, and 9, then you would have the key to the universe." The 369 method taps into this mystical power of numbers to align the mind, body, and spirit with the universe's creative energy.

Manifestation, in its essence, is the process of bringing something into your life by focusing your thoughts and energy on it. The 369 method follows a structured format where you write down what you want to manifest three times in the morning, six times in the afternoon, and nine times in the evening. This cycle is repeated for 12 consecutive days, allowing you to cultivate the right vibrational frequency and emotional alignment to draw your desires into reality. Each step of the method corresponds to the significance of the numbers 3, 6, and 9, which, when combined, are believed to hold the key to unlocking the limitless potential of the universe.

The Significance of Numbers 3, 6, and 9

In numerology, each number holds a unique vibrational frequency and symbolic meaning. The numbers 3, 6, and 9 are considered to be particularly special, representing the foundations of the universe's creative force.

- **Number 3**: The number 3 symbolizes creativity, self-expression, and communication. It is often associated with the connection between the mind, body, and spirit. In the 369 method, writing your intention three times in the morning helps activate the creative power within you, setting the tone for the day with a clear focus on what you wish to manifest. The number 3 brings forth the initial spark of creation, encouraging you to express your desires with clarity and purpose.

- **Number 6**: The number 6 is linked to harmony, balance, and nurturing. It represents love, compassion, and emotional depth. Writing your intention six times in the afternoon serves as a reinforcement, allowing you to nurture the seed of your desire. This repetition helps to solidify your belief and trust in the manifestation process, ensuring that your desire is aligned with both your heart and mind. The number 6 amplifies the emotional energy needed to bring your desire into reality, bridging the gap between intention and manifestation.

- **Number 9**: The number 9 is often associated with completion, wisdom, and spiritual enlightenment. It represents the culmination of effort and the fulfillment of one's goals. Writing your intention nine times in the evening symbolizes the final step in the creative process, where your desires move from the realm of thought into the physical world. The number 9 closes the loop of manifestation by aligning your energy with the universe's higher frequencies, allowing you to attract what you want with greater ease.

The Power of Repetition and Focus

The 369 method harnesses the power of repetition to embed your desired outcome deeply into your subconscious mind. Each repetition strengthens your belief and conviction in your ability to manifest your desires. The subconscious mind, which governs a significant portion of our thoughts and actions, is incredibly receptive to repetitive thoughts and emotions. By consistently writing down your intentions, you are essentially reprogramming your subconscious to accept your desire as truth.

Moreover, the act of writing itself is a powerful manifestation tool. When you write something down, it moves from the abstract realm of thoughts and ideas into the tangible world. This physical act of putting pen to paper creates a bridge between your internal desires and external reality. As you repeatedly write your intentions throughout the day, your focus sharpens, and your energy aligns more closely with what you want to attract.

The Importance of Emotional Alignment

Manifestation is not just about focusing on what you want; it is about aligning your emotions with the frequency of your desire. The universe responds to your emotional energy, which means that the more you feel like your desire is already yours, the faster it will come into your life. The 369 method encourages you to tap into the emotions associated with your desire. As you write down your intentions, focus on the feelings of joy, gratitude, excitement, and fulfillment that will come with receiving your desire.

For example, if you are manifesting a new job, feel the pride and accomplishment of landing your dream role as you write. If you are manifesting a loving relationship, imagine the warmth, connection, and happiness that this relationship will bring into your life. The more you can connect with these emotions, the stronger your manifestation will become.

The 12-Day Cycle: Building Momentum

The 369 method is practiced over 12 consecutive days, allowing you to build momentum and strengthen your manifestation efforts. The 12-day cycle creates a consistent practice that keeps your desire at the forefront of your mind. During this period, you may begin to notice signs from the universe that your manifestation is on its way. Synchronicities, sudden opportunities, or intuitive nudges are all common experiences during this time, as the universe aligns with your intentions.

The 12-day structure also serves as a way to keep you accountable. Manifestation requires both focus and patience, and by committing to this practice for 12 days, you are training yourself to stay focused on your desires without wavering. This level of commitment signals to the universe that you are serious about what you want, further enhancing the power of your manifestation.

The Science Behind the 369 Method

While the 369 method is deeply rooted in metaphysical principles, there is also a psychological component that supports its effectiveness. The act of writing and repeating your desires multiple times throughout the day engages your Reticular Activating System (RAS), the part of your brain responsible for filtering information. When you repeatedly focus on a specific goal or desire, your RAS begins to filter out distractions and highlights opportunities related to your manifestation. This heightened awareness allows you to recognize and act on opportunities that can bring you closer to your desired outcome.

Furthermore, by consistently focusing on what you want, you are shifting your mindset from lack to abundance. Many people unknowingly focus on what they don't have, which perpetuates a cycle of lack and frustration. The 369 method helps rewire this mindset by encouraging you to focus on what you do want, creating a positive feedback loop of thoughts, emotions, and actions that align with your desired reality.

Conclusion

The 369 Manifestation Method is a simple yet highly effective practice that combines the power of numbers, repetition, focus, and emotional alignment to help you attract your desires. Whether you are seeking to manifest love, wealth, health, or personal growth, this method provides a structured approach to align your thoughts and energy with the frequency of your desired outcome. By writing your intention three times in the morning, six times in the afternoon, and nine times at night over a 12-day period, you are tapping into the creative forces of the universe and bringing your dreams closer to reality. As you embark on your 369 manifestation journey, remember to remain open to signs from the universe, trust the process, and most importantly, believe that what you desire is already on its way to you.

History of the 369 Manifestation Method

The 369 Manifestation Method has become a popular practice among those interested in the Law of Attraction, metaphysical studies, and personal development. Though its modern prominence has largely developed in recent years, its origins are often attributed to the famous inventor and physicist, Nikola Tesla. Tesla's connection to the numbers 3, 6, and 9 forms the philosophical and mystical basis of the 369 Method, which is now widely used by people around the world to manifest their desires. However, the history of the 369 Method is not limited to Tesla alone. Its roots can be traced through various traditions, scientific theories, and esoteric practices, each contributing to the development of this potent manifestation tool.

Nikola Tesla and the Mystical Significance of 3, 6, and 9

The modern foundation of the 369 Method is intricately tied to the work and beliefs of Nikola Tesla. Tesla, one of the greatest minds in history, is known for his groundbreaking inventions and pioneering work in the field of electricity and magnetism. However, beyond his scientific achievements, Tesla was also deeply spiritual and fascinated by numerology, cosmic energy, and the mysteries of the universe.

Tesla is famously quoted as saying, "If you only knew the magnificence of the numbers 3, 6, and 9, you would have the key to the universe." This enigmatic statement has been the subject of much interpretation and speculation, but Tesla's reverence for these numbers was rooted in his belief that they held a universal significance beyond their mathematical properties.

- **The Number 3**: Tesla saw the number 3 as representing the fundamental aspects of existence, including the triad of energy, frequency, and vibration—concepts central to his scientific work. He also associated the number 3 with the trinity of creation, preservation, and destruction, found in various spiritual traditions, symbolizing the cycles of life.
- **The Number 6**: For Tesla, the number 6 represented balance and harmony. In the context of numerology and spiritual understanding, 6 is often seen as the number of responsibility and nurturing. It plays a significant role in keeping the flow of energy balanced, which Tesla believed was crucial to understanding the universe.
- **The Number 9**: Tesla considered the number 9 the most important of all, seeing it as the number of completion and universal energy. In numerology, 9 is the culmination of all the previous numbers, symbolizing wisdom, enlightenment, and the comple-

tion of cycles. Tesla believed that the number 9 was the key to unlocking the mysteries of the universe, as it held a unique connection to higher dimensions of existence.

Tesla's fascination with these numbers was not merely academic; he reportedly incorporated them into his daily life. For instance, he would often walk around buildings three times before entering, or he would perform activities in multiples of three. Tesla believed that these numbers were tied to the fabric of reality and that understanding them could unlock the secrets of the cosmos.

Numerology and the Power of Repetition

Although Tesla popularized the significance of 3, 6, and 9, the use of numbers in mystical practices has been prevalent in various cultures throughout history. Numerology, the study of the mystical significance of numbers, has long been used as a tool for understanding the universe, human behavior, and the connection between the spiritual and physical realms. In numerology, numbers are believed to carry vibrational frequencies that influence different aspects of life. The practice of using specific numbers for manifestation, rituals, and prayer can be traced back to ancient civilizations.

- **Pythagoras and Ancient Greece**: The ancient Greek mathematician Pythagoras was one of the earliest figures to explore the spiritual significance of numbers. Pythagoras and his followers believed that the universe operated according to numerical relationships and that numbers held symbolic meanings. Pythagoras considered 3 to be the perfect number, representing harmony, wisdom, and understanding. The concept of a triad, or three-part structure, was fundamental in Pythagorean philosophy, and this idea heavily influenced the use of numbers in spiritual practices.
- **Sacred Texts and Traditions**: Many religious and spiritual traditions place significant importance on the repetition of numbers. In Christianity, the number 3 is often associated with the Holy Trinity (Father, Son, and Holy Spirit). In Hinduism, the Trimurti represents the triad of the gods Brahma (the creator), Vishnu (the preserver), and Shiva (the destroyer). Similarly, in Buddhism, the number 9 holds sacred value as it symbolizes the Nine Realms of Existence. These spiritual traditions show that the use of numbers in sacred rituals is a practice rooted in ancient history.

Repetition itself is also an essential element in many manifestation techniques, including the 369 Method. The act of repeating mantras, prayers, or affirmations is common in a variety of spiritual practices. This repetition is believed to reinforce beliefs, clear mental blocks, and align the individual with their desires. The power of repetition is psychological as well as spiritual, as it ingrains the desired outcome into the subconscious mind, making it more likely to manifest in the physical world.

The Law of Attraction and the Emergence of the 369 Method
The rise of the 369 Manifestation Method can also be linked to the modern popularity of the Law of Attraction, a metaphysical philosophy that emphasizes the power of thoughts and beliefs in shaping one's reality. The Law of Attraction gained significant attention in the 19th and 20th centuries, particularly through the New Thought movement, which emphasized the power of positive thinking, visualization, and the ability to attract what one desires.

In 2006, the documentary and book **"The Secret"** popularized the Law of Attraction, bringing it into mainstream consciousness. The core premise of the Law of Attraction is that like attracts like, meaning that the thoughts, feelings, and beliefs we hold about ourselves and the world create our reality. Manifestation techniques, including the 369 Method, are rooted in this principle, using focused thought and intention to attract desired outcomes.

The 369 Method itself is a relatively modern manifestation technique, but it draws upon the principles of both the Law of Attraction and Tesla's belief in the power of 3, 6, and 9. By repeating a specific desire or intention in multiples of 3, 6, and 9, the practitioner is believed to align their energy with the frequency of their desire, making it more likely to manifest.

The Role of the Subconscious Mind

One of the key elements behind the success of the 369 Method is its ability to engage the subconscious mind. Modern psychology has shown that the subconscious mind is responsible for a large portion of our thoughts, behaviors, and habits. Repeatedly writing down one's desires in the 369 Method helps to reprogram the subconscious mind, aligning it with the desired outcome. This practice shifts the individual's beliefs and energy, making it easier for them to notice opportunities, take action, and attract the desired result.

The repetitive structure of the 369 Method ensures that the practitioner remains focused on their goal throughout the day, helping to build momentum and reinforce their belief in the manifestation process. Over time, the subconscious mind begins to accept the desired outcome as a reality, influencing the individual's thoughts, actions, and circumstances in ways that bring them closer to their goal.

Modern Adaptations and Popularity

In the age of social media, the 369 Method has experienced a resurgence in popularity, especially within the self-help and spiritual communities. Platforms like TikTok, Instagram, and YouTube have played a significant role in spreading the practice, with users sharing their experiences and success stories. The simplicity of the 369 Method, combined with its ties to Tesla's mystique, has made it a favorite among those looking to manifest their desires in a structured and effective way.

The method is now often used for a wide variety of manifestations, including love, financial abundance, career success, and personal growth. While the original focus was on repetition and alignment with universal energy, modern practitioners have also incorporated additional elements such as visualization, gratitude, and emotional alignment to enhance the manifestation process.

Conclusion

The 369 Manifestation Method is a synthesis of ancient numerology, spiritual practices, and modern metaphysical philosophies. Its history is rooted in the esoteric teachings of Nikola Tesla, whose fascination with the numbers 3, 6, and 9 inspired the development of this powerful manifestation technique. Over time, the method has evolved, blending principles of the Law of Attraction, psychology, and spiritual repetition to become a widely used tool for personal transformation.

Today, the 369 Method continues to resonate with people across the globe, offering a simple yet profound way to align thoughts, emotions, and actions with their deepest desires. As the method continues to evolve, its core principle remains timeless: through focused intention, repetition, and belief, individuals can tap into the creative forces of the universe and bring their dreams into reality.

The Power of 12 in Manifestation and the 369 Method

The number 12 has a deep and mystical significance across various cultures, spiritual traditions, and scientific principles. It has long been regarded as a symbol of completion, divine order, and cosmic balance. In the context of the 369 Manifestation Method, the addition of a 12-day cycle amplifies the power of the original method, allowing for greater alignment with universal energies and a more profound connection to one's desires. To understand why 12 is so powerful in manifestation, it's essential to explore its numerological, spiritual, and scientific meanings, and how it complements the numbers 3, 6, and 9, as emphasized by Nikola Tesla.

The Significance of 12 in Numerology and Spiritual Traditions

In numerology, the number 12 is considered a master number, representing wholeness, perfection, and the completion of cycles. It is often seen as a number that bridges the material and spiritual realms, symbolizing cosmic harmony. The number 12 appears throughout human history and spiritual traditions as a symbol of order and divine structure. Some notable examples include:

- **The 12 Zodiac Signs**: In astrology, the 12 zodiac signs represent different aspects of human experience and personality, forming a complete cycle of life's spiritual journey.
- **The 12 Months of the Year**: The Gregorian calendar, used in most parts of the world, is based on a 12-month cycle, which divides the solar year. This division represents the cyclical nature of time, mirroring the cosmic order.
- **The 12 Labors of Hercules**: In Greek mythology, Hercules completed 12 labors, symbolizing the hero's journey through trials and tribulations to attain spiritual enlightenment.

Throughout history, 12 has been seen as a number of balance, reflecting both physical and spiritual realities. Its presence in religious, mythological, and astrological systems highlights its role as a number that governs completeness and the cyclical nature of life.

The Mathematical and Scientific Significance of 12

Beyond spiritual and cultural meanings, the number 12 also holds mathematical and scientific importance. It is considered a highly divisible number, as it can be divided evenly by 1, 2, 3, 4, 6, and 12. This divisibility allows for balance and order, which is why the number 12 appears so frequently in measurements and timekeeping systems.

- **The Base-12 System**: Historically, many ancient cultures used a base-12 counting system. For example, the Babylonians developed a system based on 12, which influenced modern-day timekeeping. We divide our days into two 12-hour periods, measure our years in 12 months, and track the passage of time with 12 major intervals on a clock.
- **The 12-Tone Musical Scale**: In music theory, the 12-tone scale is the basis for Western musical composition. The number 12 is seen as the perfect cycle for creating harmony and musical structure.

The mathematical properties of 12 reinforce its association with order, harmony, and structure. These qualities make 12 an ideal number to incorporate into the 369 Manifestation Method, as it adds a sense of completion and finality to the process.

Nikola Tesla and the Power of 3, 6, 9 — Expanding to 12

Nikola Tesla, one of the most brilliant and enigmatic minds in history, was deeply fascinated by the power of numbers, especially 3, 6, and 9. He believed that these numbers held the key to understanding the universe's hidden patterns, often referring to them as the "code" to unlocking the mysteries of existence.

Tesla's fixation on 3, 6, and 9 was based on the idea that these numbers are integral to the structure of the universe. He believed that everything in the universe operates according to energy, frequency, and vibration, and that these three numbers were central to this universal code.

Why Tesla Believed 3, 6, and 9 Were Powerful:

1. **Number 3**: Tesla considered 3 to be the fundamental building block of the universe. It represents the triad, which appears in various forms across science, spirituality, and nature. For example, light can be divided into three primary colors (red, green, and blue), and matter can exist in three states (solid, liquid, gas). In spiritual traditions, 3 represents the trinity—mind, body, and spirit. Tesla believed that the number 3 governed creation and the initial stages of manifestation.

2. **Number 6**: The number 6, according to Tesla, represents the balance and harmonization of energies. It symbolizes the connection between the physical and spiritual realms. Tesla saw the number 6 as integral to maintaining equilibrium in the universe. In the 369 Method, writing down your manifestation six times aligns you with the emotional and energetic balance needed to bring your desire into reality.

3. **Number 9**: Tesla considered 9 to be the most powerful number in the universe, symbolizing completion, enlightenment, and universal energy. He believed that 9 held the key to understanding the higher dimensions and that it was the final step in the manifestation process. The number 9 closes the loop of creation and brings desires into the physical realm. Tesla saw 9 as the "universal frequency" that connected everything in the cosmos.

By expanding the 369 method to a 12-day cycle, practitioners are effectively tapping into the full spectrum of Tesla's numerical insights while also incorporating the cosmic completeness of 12. The number 12 acts as the structural framework within which the 369 energies operate. It adds an additional layer of power, reinforcing the manifestation process through the combination of divine order and cosmic timing.

The Synergy Between 369 and 12

Incorporating a 12-day cycle into the 369 Method further enhances the manifestation process by aligning it with both spiritual and physical principles. Here's why the combination of 3, 6, 9, and 12 creates such a potent manifestation tool:

1. **The Power of Cycles**: The universe operates in cycles, from the moon's phases to the changing seasons. A 12-day cycle mirrors this natural rhythm and allows for a manifestation process that aligns with the flow of the universe. By practicing the 369 method for 12 consecutive days, you are working in harmony with these universal cycles, reinforcing your intentions and creating momentum.

2. **Reinforcement of Intention**: The 12-day cycle ensures that your intention is consistently reinforced over time. Repetition is key to manifestation because it impresses your desire onto your subconscious mind, which governs your beliefs, thoughts, and actions. The structure of 12 days allows enough time for your subconscious mind to fully absorb the message and align with your desired outcome.

3. **Completion and Integration**: The number 12 symbolizes completion, making the end of the 12-day cycle a powerful moment of integration. After completing the 12 days, your mind, body, and spirit are fully aligned with your manifestation. The energy of 12 helps to solidify your desire in the physical realm, completing the process and allowing it to manifest in your reality.

The Scientific Basis for 369, 12

In addition to its spiritual and numerological significance, the 369, 12 combination has a psychological and neurological basis. Repeating affirmations or desires over a 12-day period engages the brain's Reticular Activating System (RAS), the part of the brain responsible for filtering information and focusing attention. By consistently writing down your desire in multiples of 3, 6, and 9 for 12 days, you are training your brain to focus on opportunities and actions that align with your goal. The 12-day cycle gives your brain enough time to rewire itself and shift your perspective toward your desired outcome.

Conclusion: The Power of 369, 12 in Manifestation

The combination of 3, 6, 9, and 12 in the manifestation process is a powerful synthesis of numerology, spiritual traditions, and modern psychology. Nikola Tesla's insights into the power of 3, 6, and 9 provide the foundation for understanding the universe's hidden patterns, while the number 12 amplifies these energies by aligning the manifestation process with the cycles of completion and cosmic order.

When practiced over a 12-day period, the 369 Method creates a strong, harmonious connection between the practitioner's desires and the universal energy. It uses the creative force of 3, the balance of 6, the completion of 9, and the cosmic alignment of 12 to manifest desires with clarity, focus, and emotional alignment.

By working with these numbers in a structured format, individuals are able to bring their thoughts, emotions, and actions into alignment with their desires, making the manifestation process more powerful and effective. The 369, 12 combination serves as a key to unlocking one's full manifestation potential, allowing them to create the reality they desire in harmony with the universe's natural rhythms.

Extensive and Detailed Instructions on How to Use the 369, 12 Manifestation Journal

Welcome to the **369, 12 Manifestation Journal**, a powerful tool designed to help you align with your desires and manifest your dreams into reality. This journal is based on the **369 Method**, inspired by the work of Nikola Tesla, and expanded to include a **12-day cycle** to maximize its effectiveness. The journal combines the power of numbers, repetition, intention, and emotional alignment to tap into the universal energy that governs manifestation. By following this step-by-step guide, you'll learn how to effectively use this journal to manifest your deepest desires.

What You'll Need:

- A dedicated journal or notebook
- A pen (preferably one you use only for this purpose)
- A quiet space where you can focus without distractions

Step-by-Step Guide to Using the 369, 12 Manifestation Journal

1. **Define Your Desire (Before Starting the 12 Days)**
   - Before you begin the 12-day cycle, spend some time reflecting on what you want to manifest. Be specific, clear, and focused. Write down your desire as if it has already happened, using the present tense. For example, instead of writing "I want to be financially successful," write "I am financially abundant and live in prosperity."
   - Ensure that your desire resonates deeply with you. Feel the emotions associated with having already achieved it, whether it's joy, gratitude, or excitement. The more emotion you can infuse into your desire, the more powerful your manifestation will be.
2. **Day 1 to Day 12: The 369 Writing Practice**
   - **Morning (Write Your Desire 3 Times):**
     - Every morning, shortly after waking up, take your journal and write your desire down **3 times**. Focus on the clarity of your intention as you write. Take a few moments to close your eyes and visualize your desire as if it is already manifesting. Feel the emotions connected to it—whether it's joy, peace, love, or gratitude. Writing your desire first thing in the morning sets the tone for the day, aligning your energy with your goal.
     - Example: "I am financially abundant, living a life of prosperity and freedom."
   - **Afternoon (Write Your Desire 6 Times):**
     - In the afternoon, find a quiet moment to write your desire down **6 times**. At this stage, you're reinforcing the intention you set earlier in the day. Writing it more times deepens the emotional connection and

strengthens the belief that your desire is coming to fruition. Repetition builds energy around your goal, making it more powerful with each iteration.

- As you write, take a moment after each entry to reflect on how it feels to already have what you desire. The more vividly you can imagine it, the more aligned your energy will become with your manifestation.

- Example: "I am financially abundant, living a life of prosperity and freedom."

- **Evening (Write Your Desire 9 Times)**:
  - Before going to bed, write your desire down **9 times**. The evening writing session is crucial, as it taps into the subconscious mind just before you sleep. During sleep, the subconscious processes information and plays a significant role in creating your reality. By writing your desire down 9 times, you're embedding it deeply into your subconscious mind, which helps accelerate the manifestation process.

  - After writing your entries, take a few moments to meditate or visualize your desire once again, feeling as though it has already happened. Allow the emotions of gratitude, joy, and excitement to wash over you.

  - Example: "I am financially abundant, living a life of prosperity and freedom."

3. **Reflect on Your Day (Nightly Routine)**
   - After completing your 9 evening entries, take a few minutes to **read your entries for the day** before going to bed. As you read them, focus on the feeling that your desire is already manifesting. This simple act helps to further solidify your belief that what you desire is already yours.

- This nightly reading helps **program your subconscious mind** just before sleep. The subconscious mind is most receptive during these moments, as it processes thoughts and emotions from the day during the dream state. By repeatedly exposing your subconscious to your desired outcome, you're creating new neural pathways that support your manifestation. Over time, your subconscious mind begins to believe that your desire is already a reality, aligning your thoughts, actions, and opportunities to make it come true.

4. **Consistency Over 12 Days**
   - Repeat this process for **12 consecutive days**. The 12-day cycle represents completion, balance, and cosmic order. By committing to this process for 12 days, you are signaling to the universe and your subconscious mind that you are serious about manifesting your desires. The 12-day repetition builds momentum and strengthens your manifestation energy.
   - Be patient and trust the process. Manifestation is not just about writing things down; it's about aligning your energy with your desires. This means trusting that the universe is working in your favor, even if you don't see immediate results.

Understanding the Power of Reading Before Bed

The reason why it's important to **read your entries before bed** is that this practice taps into the power of the **subconscious mind**. The subconscious mind is responsible for a significant portion of your thoughts, beliefs, and behaviors. It operates 24/7, even when you are asleep, processing the information it receives throughout the day. By focusing on your desires just before you sleep, you are "feeding" your subconscious with positive, goal-oriented thoughts.

When you go to bed with your manifestation in mind, your subconscious works to align your beliefs and actions with that desire. Over time, your subconscious mind starts to remove the mental and emotional barriers that might be preventing your manifestation from becoming reality. This is why people often experience unexpected opportunities, synchronicities, or "aha" moments when using this method—it's the subconscious mind attracting the right circumstances to bring your desires to fruition.

By reading your manifestation statements just before sleep, you:

- **Strengthen your belief** in your desire's eventual manifestation.
- **Reprogram your subconscious mind** to focus on the positive outcomes you want, rather than on fears or doubts.
- **Create a mental environment** that attracts opportunities, ideas, and actions aligned with your goal.
- **Reinforce emotional alignment**, ensuring that you go to sleep with feelings of gratitude, excitement, and confidence.

Additional Tips for Success

1. **Visualize**: Along with writing your desires, make it a habit to **visualize your goal** as if it has already happened. Create a clear mental picture of what your life looks like after your manifestation has occurred. Visualization, combined with writing, creates a powerful energetic connection to your desire.
2. **Gratitude**: Each day, after writing your entries, practice gratitude for the things you already have. Gratitude raises your vibration, putting you in a positive state that is more conducive to attracting what you want. It also shows the universe that you appreciate what you already have, making you more open to receiving more.
3. **Let Go of the 'How'**: While it's important to be clear about what you want, don't worry about **how** it will come into your life. Trust that the universe will arrange the perfect circumstances for your manifestation. Focus on the 'what' and 'why,' and let the universe handle the 'how.'
4. **Stay Open to Signs**: During the 12 days, pay attention to signs, synchronicities, and opportunities that may arise. These could be subtle nudges from the universe guiding you toward your manifestation. Be ready to take inspired action when these signs appear.
5. **Maintain a Positive Mindset**: As you go through the 12 days, maintain a positive and optimistic mindset. Avoid focusing on doubts, fears, or negative thoughts. If they arise, gently shift your focus back to your desired outcome.

Completion of the 12 Days

At the end of the 12 days, take time to **reflect on your journey**. Review your entries, meditate on the emotions and growth you experienced, and acknowledge any signs of progress or manifestation that may have appeared. This reflection helps to solidify your belief that your manifestation is unfolding in perfect timing.

While some manifestations may occur quickly, others may take time. Trust that the seeds you've planted during these 12 days are growing, even if you cannot yet see the results. The 369, 12 method is designed to align your thoughts, feelings, and energy with your desires, creating a new reality where your goals are achievable and within reach.

By following these steps with consistency, focus, and belief, you are actively shaping your reality and aligning yourself with the universal energy that governs all creation.

By incorporating this detailed process, you ensure that each part of your manifestation is carefully nurtured, from setting your initial intention to embedding it deeply into your subconscious mind.

Day 1
Goals:

How will you treat yourself today

Morning (Write your desire 3 times):

1.____

2.____

3.____

Afternoon (Write your desire 6 times):

1.____

2.____

3.____

4.____

5.____

6.____

Night (Write your desire 9 times):

1. ____

2. ____

3. ____

4. ____

5. ____

6. ____

7. ____

8. ____

9. ____

"What you think, you create. What you feel, you attract. What you imagine, you become." – Anonymous

Trust in the power of your mind to shape your reality.

<u>Day 2</u>
Goals:

How will you treat yourself today:

Morning (Write your desire 3 times):

1.____

2.____

3.____

Afternoon (Write your desire 6 times):

1.____

2.____

3.____

4.____

5.____

6.____

Night (Write your desire 9 times):

1.____

2.____

3.____

4.____

5.____

6.____

7.____

8.____

9.____

"The universe is not outside of you. Look inside yourself; everything that you want, you already are." – Rumi

Remember, the key to manifestation lies within you.

Day 3

Goals:

How will you treat yourself today:

Morning (Write your desire 3 times):

1.____________________________________

2.____________________________________

3.____________________________________

Afternoon (Write your desire 6 times):

1.____________________________________

2.____________________________________

3.____________________________________

4.____________________________________

5.____________________________________

6.____________________________________

Night (Write your desire 9 times):

1.____________________________________

2.____________________________________

3.____________________________________

4.____________________________________

5.____________________________________

6.____________________________________

7.____________________________________

8.____________________________________

9.____________________________________

"Ask for what you want and be prepared to get it." – Maya Angelou

Believe that the universe is ready to deliver your desires when you're open to receiving them.

Day 4
Goals:

How will you treat yourself today:

Morning (Write your desire 3 times):

1.____

2.____

3.____

Afternoon (Write your desire 6 times):

1.____

2.____

3.____

4.____

5.____

6.____

Night (Write your desire 9 times):

1.____

2.____

3.____

4.____

5.____

6.____

7.____

8.____

9.____

You don't manifest what you want, you manifest what you believe." – Neville Goddard

Align your beliefs with your desires to make them a reality.

<u>Day 5</u>
Goals:

How will you treat yourself today

Morning (Write your desire 3 times):

1.____

2.____

3.____

Afternoon (Write your desire 6 times):

1.____

2.____

3.____

4.____

5.____

6.____

Night (Write your desire 9 times):

1.____

2.____

3.____

4.____

5.____

6.____

7.____

8.____

9.____

"The only limits to your success are the ones you place on yourself." – Anonymous

Release self-doubt and open your mind to infinite possibilities.

__Day 6__
Goals:

How will you treat yourself today:

Morning (Write your desire 3 times):

1.____

2.____

3.____

Afternoon (Write your desire 6 times):

1.____

2.____

3.____

4.____

5.____

6.____

Night (Write your desire 9 times):

1.____

2.____

3.____

4.____

5.____

6.____

7.____

8.____

9.____

"Act as if what you intend to manifest is already true, and the universe will reflect your belief back to you." – Wayne Dyer

Embrace the energy of having what you desire now, and the universe will mirror it.

Day 7
Goals:

How will you treat yourself today:

Morning (Write your desire 3 times):

1.____

2.____

3.____

Afternoon (Write your desire 6 times):

1.____

2.____

3.____

4.____

5.____

6.____

Night (Write your desire 9 times):

1.____

2.____

3.____

4.____

5.____

6.____

7.____

8.____

9.____

"Your energy is your currency. Spend it wisely, invest in what you want to create." – Anonymous

Focus your energy on your dreams, and watch them grow.

<u>Day 8</u>
Goals:

How will you treat yourself today:

Morning (Write your desire 3 times):

1.____

2.____

3.____

Afternoon (Write your desire 6 times):

1.____

2.____

3.____

4.____

5.____

6.____

Night (Write your desire 9 times):

1.____

2.____

3.____

4.____

5.____

6.____

7.____

8.____

9.____

"Everything you can imagine is real." – Pablo Picasso

If you can visualize it, you have the power to manifest it.

Day 9
Goals:

How will you treat yourself today:

Morning (Write your desire 3 times):

1.__________________________________

2.__________________________________

3.__________________________________

Afternoon (Write your desire 6 times):

1.__________________________________

2.__________________________________

3.__________________________________

4.__________________________________

5.__________________________________

6.__________________________________

Night (Write your desire 9 times):

1.______________________________________

2.______________________________________

3.______________________________________

4.______________________________________

5.______________________________________

6.______________________________________

7.______________________________________

8.______________________________________

9.______________________________________

"Believe in the power of the unseen. The universe works behind the scenes to bring your dreams to life." – Anonymous

Have faith in the unseen forces that are always working in your favor.

<u>Day 10</u>
Goals:

How will you treat yourself today:

Morning (Write your desire 3 times):

1.____

2.____

3.____

Afternoon (Write your desire 6 times):

1.____

2.____

3.____

4.____

5.____

6.____

Night (Write your desire 9 times):

1.____

2.____

3.____

4.____

5.____

6.____

7.____

8.____

9.____

"The secret to manifesting is simple: hold the vision, trust the process." – Anonymous

Stay committed to your vision and trust that it is on its way.

<u>Day 11</u>
Goals:

How will you treat yourself today:

Morning (Write your desire 3 times):

1.____

2.____

3.____

Afternoon (Write your desire 6 times):

1.____

2.____

3.____

4.____

5.____

6.____

Night (Write your desire 9 times):

1.____

2.____

3.____

4.____

5.____

6.____

7.____

8.____

9.____

"Gratitude is the magic key to manifesting your desires. Be thankful now for what is yet to come." – Rhonda Byrne

Cultivate gratitude for your desires as if they have already arrived.

<u>Day 12</u>
Goals:

How will you treat yourself today:

Morning (Write your desire 3 times):

1.____

2.____

3.____

Afternoon (Write your desire 6 times):

1.____

2.____

3.____

4.____

5.____

6.____

Night (Write your desire 9 times):

1.____

2.____

3.____

4.____

5.____

6.____

7.____

8.____

9.____

You are the creator of your own destiny. What you focus on expands." – Oprah Winfrey

Keep your focus on what you want, and watch your dreams unfold.

Reflections:

1. How did writing your manifestations each day make you feel?

2. What changes have you noticed in your mindset or actions during these 12 days?

3.Are there any signs or synchronicities that suggest your manifestation is coming to fruition?

4.What steps can you take next to align further with your manifestation?

<u>Message from the Author:</u>

I hope you enjoyed this book, I love astrology and knew there was not a book such as this out on the shelf. I love metaphysical items as well. Please check out my other books:

-Life of Government Benefits

-My life of Hell

-My life with Hydrocephalus

-Red Sky

-World Domination:Woman's rule

-World Domination:Woman's Rule 2: The War

-Life and Banishment of Apophis: book 1

-The Kidney Friendly Diet

-The Ultimate Hemp Cookbook

-Creating a Dispensary(legally)

-Cleanliness throughout life: the importance of showering from childhood to adulthood.

-Strong Roots: The Risks of Overcoddling children

-Hemp Horoscopes: Cosmic Insights and Earthly Healing

- Celestial Hemp Navigating the Zodiac: Through the Green Cosmos

-Astrological Hemp: Aligning The Stars with Earth's Ancient Herb

-The Astrological Guide to Hemp: Stars, Signs, and Sacred Leaves

-Green Growth: Innovative Marketing Strategies for your Hemp Products and Dispensary

-Cosmic Cannabis

-Astrological Munchies

-Henry The Hemp

-Zodiacal Roots: The Astrological Soul Of Hemp

- **Green Constellations: Intersection of Hemp and Zodiac**

-Hemp in The Houses: An astrological Adventure Through The Cannabis Galaxy

-Galactic Ganja Guide

Heavenly Hemp

Zodiac Leaves

Doctor Who Astrology

Cannastrology

Stellar Satvias and Cosmic Indicas

<u>Celestial Cannabis: A Zodiac Journey</u>

AstroHerbology: The Sky and The Soil: Volume 1

AstroHerbology:Celestial Cannabis:Volume 2

Cosmic Cannabis Cultivation

The Starry Guide to Herbal Harmony: Volume 1

The Starry Guide to Herbal Harmony: Cannabis Universe: Volume 2

Yugioh Astrology: Astrological Guide to Deck, Duels and more

Nightmare Mansion: Echoes of The Abyss

Nightmare Mansion 2: Legacy of Shadows

Nightmare Mansion 3: Shadows of the Forgotten

Nightmare Mansion 4: Echoes of the Damned

The Life and Banishment of Apophis: Book 2

Nightmare Mansion: Halls of Despair

<u>Healing with Herb: Cannabis and Hydrocephalus</u>

<u>Planetary Pot: Aligning with Astrological Herbs: Volume 1</u>

Fast Track to Freedom: 30 Days to Financial Independence Using AI, Assets, and Agile Hustles

<u>Cosmic Hemp Pathways</u>

How to Become Financially Free in 30 Days: 10,000 Paths to Prosperity

Zodiacal Herbage: Astrological Insights: Volume 1

Nightmare Mansion: Whispers in the Walls

The Daleks Invade Atlantis

Henry the hemp and Hydrocephalus

10X The Kidney Friendly Diet

Cannabis Universe: Adult coloring book

Hemp Astrology: The Healing Power of the Stars

Zodiacal Herbage: Astrological Insights: Cannabis Universe: Volume 2

<u>**Planetary Pot: Aligning with Astrological Herbs: Cannabis Universes: Volume 2**</u>

Doctor Who Meets the Replicators and SG-1: The Ultimate Battle for Survival

Nightmare Mansion: Curse of the Blood Moon

<u>**The Celestial Stoner: A Guide to the Zodiac**</u>

Cosmic Pleasures: Sex Toy Astrology for Every Sign

Hydrocephalus Astrology: Navigating the Stars and Healing Waters

Lapis and the Mischievous Chocolate Bar

Celestial Positions: Sexual Astrology for Every Sign

Apophis's Shadow Work Journal: : A Journey of Self-Discovery and Healing

Kinky Cosmos: Sexual Kink Astrology for Every Sign

Digital Cosmos: The Astrological Digimon Compendium

Stellar Seeds: The Cosmic Guide to Growing with Astrology

Apophis's Daily Gratitude Journal

Cat Astrology: Feline Mysteries of the Cosmos

The Cosmic Kama Sutra: An Astrological Guide to Sexual Positions

Unleash Your Potential: A Guided Journal Powered by AI Insights

Whispers of the Enchanted Grove

Cosmic Pleasures: An Astrological Guide to Sexual Kinks

If you want solar for your home go here: https://www.harborso-lar.live/apophisenterprises/

Get Some Tarot cards: https://www.makeplayingcards.com/sell/apophis-occult-shop

<u>Get some shirts: https://www.bonfire.com/store/apophis-shirt-emporium/</u>

<u>Instagrams:</u>
@apophis_enterprises,
@apophisbookemporium,
@apophisscardshop

Twitter: @apophisenterpr1

Tiktok:@apophisenterprise

Youtube: @sg1fan23477, @FiresideRetreatKingdom Top of Form

Podcast: Apophis Chat Zone: https://open.spotify.com/show/5zXbrCLEV2xzCp8ybrfHsk?si=fb4d4fdbdce44dec

Newsletter: https://apophiss-newsletter-27c897.beehiiv.com/

www.ingramcontent.com/pod-product-compliance
Lightning Source LLC
Chambersburg PA
CBHW061311140726
47998CB00006B/2346

9 798333 030084 6